DEPARTMENT OF THE NAVY
HEADQUARTERS UNITED STATES MARINE CORPS
3280 RUSSELL ROAD
QUANTICO, VIRGINIA 22134-5103

PERFORMANCE MANAGEMENT PROGRAM

DEPARTMENT OF THE NAVY
HEADQUARTERS UNITED STATES MARINE CORPS
3280 RUSSELL ROAD
QUANTICO, VIRGINIA 22134-5103

MCO 12430.2
MPO-30
29 DEC 1998

MARINE CORPS ORDER 12430.2

From: Commandant of the Marine Corps
To: Distribution List

Subj: PERFORMANCE MANAGEMENT PROGRAM

Ref: (a) SECNAVINST 12430.4
      (b) DoD 1400.25-M, Subchapter 430, Performance Management
      (c) MCO 12451.2C
      (d) SECNAVINST 12451.3
      (e) MCO 12421.24

Encl: (1) Performance Appraisal Review System (NAVMC 11408 (9-98)) EF
      (2) Examples of Critical Elements
      (3) Additional Performance Requirements
      (4) Elements Rating Conversion Chart

1. <u>Purpose</u>. To provide policy and responsibility for civilian performance management and a formal Performance Appraisal Review System (PARS) within the Marine Corps.

2. <u>Background</u>. Reference (a) establishes a two-level summary rating program for Department of the Navy. Reference (b) is Department of Defense amplifying instructions for establishing performance management within the military services.

3. <u>Effective date</u>. 1 October 1998.

4. <u>Policy</u>. All performance management programs used within the Marine Corps will be two-level summary rating programs as defined in references (a) and (b) effective with the 1998-1999 performance rating periods. Performance management is an essential element of Marine Corps policy to recognize civilian employee standards of excellence and provide a system of recognition for work well done. To acknowledge employees accomplishments above normal expectations of performance of duties, commanders shall make every effort to use the mode of rewards found in references (c) and (d). It is important to recognize employee contributions to the Marine Corps and the unit mission thereby fostering attitudes of excellence to develop leaders for the 21st Century. Promotions and hiring for positions are dependent on the excellence of the employees' contributions.

DISTRIBUTION STATEMENT A: Approved for public release; distribution is unlimited.

a. The following is policy for implementation:

(1) The appraisal performance rating levels are "Acceptable or Unacceptable."

(2) Enclosure (1) will be used in evaluating the performance of all civilian employees in the Marine Corps. Electronic form access is available.

(3) Reduction-in-force (RIF) policy is provided in detail in paragraph 13e of this order.

(4) Enclosure (2) provides examples of statements that would be appropriate for Critical Elements for performance appraisal.

(5) Critical elements in the performance appraisal shall include specific technical, security, or supervisory performance required of the employee as described under additional performance requirements at enclosure (3).

5. Applicability. This Order applies to all appropriated fund employees of the Marine Corps excluding Senior Executive Service. This Order does not apply to nonappropriated fund employees, employees outside the United States paid in accordance with local national prevailing wage rates for the area in which employed; individuals appointed by the President; employees occupying excepted service positions not to exceed the minimum performance period established in a consecutive 12 month period; employees under a temporary appointment for less than 1 year, who agree to serve without a performance evaluation, and who will not be considered for reappointment or for an increase in pay based in whole or in part on performance; and individuals excluded from coverage under other applicable law.

6. General Instructions

a. Performance management will involve employees in improving organizational effectiveness and in assessing individual employee team, effectiveness and performance;

b. Involve employees in program development and implementation;

c. Performance management programs and employee work plans will be designed to integrate management processes that:

(1) Communicate and clarify mission, organizational goals and objectives.

(2) Identify employee, team and managerial accountability for the accomplishment of goals and objectives;

(3) Use appropriate measures to recognize and reward employees and use the results of performance appraisal as a basis for appropriate personnel actions;

(4) Encourage employees to take responsibility for continuous improvement, support team endeavors, develop professionally and perform at their full potential.

7. <u>Actions</u>

   a. Marine Corps activity heads or commanders where applicable will:

   (1) Establish a performance management program and implementing instructions in accordance with this Order and references (a) and (b).

   (2) Establish a beginning and ending rating period based on the calendar year most appropriate for their activity.

   (3) Oversee the PARS and the incentive award and monetary reward process.

   (4) Establish a Performance Review Board or appoint a senior Reviewing Official to review "Unacceptable" performance appraisals. The Review Board or Reviewing Official shall ensure standards have been applied equitably, a plan of improvement was provided by the supervisor to the employee in a timely manner and ensure management made efforts to assist the employee to improve performance to an "Acceptable" level. If upon review, the employee performance is still considered Unacceptable", then the activity will initiate a personnel action of reduction in grade, reassignment, removal or other appropriate personnel action.

   (5) Ensure supervisors fulfill their obligations under the Federal Service Labor-Management Relations Statue, Chapter 71 of Title 5, U.S.C., to fulfill any requirements for collective bargaining prior to implementation. The Marine Corps Master Labor Agreement (MLA) is the primary policy authority where appropriate. Point of contact is CMC (MPO-37) for questions concerning the MLA.

(6) Strongly emphasize the use of references (c) and (d) to commanders and supervisors as the guidance for recognizing excellence of employee performance.

(7) See that appropriate training is provided to personnel who supervise civilian employees and manage the performance appraisal program at commands under their authority.

(8) Appoint activity head designees to review and act as approving authority for performance award nominations; to include quality step increases (QSI) submitted by their activity.

(9) Ensure enclosure (1) is available to all supervisors and managers for appraising employees performance. It shall include a minimum of two critical elements concerning work performance. For those employees who work in teams for completion of projects, at least one critical element shall be a team member performance appraisal element; not an evaluation for the team. Evaluate team member performance only on those work objectives of the individual employee. There shall also be at least one critical element each for supervisory responsibilities or managerial responsibilities. Enclosure (2) is sample critical elements.

   b. Commanders will:

(1) Ensure performance appraisals are completed on schedule for each eligible employee for the period set by the activity head. Supervisors and managers must be accountable for getting the employees appraisal completed on time. All appraisals will be completed or reviewed as required for "Unacceptable" performance within 60 days of the close of the performance period.

(2) Ensure supervisors, managers and team leaders are aware of the importance of the reward system as a means of distinguishing employees' excellent performance from "Acceptable" performance of duty. Time off and cash spot awards are examples of rewards.

(3) Ensure employees rated at the "Unacceptable" performance level are counseled by their supervisor as soon as the unacceptable performance presents itself and before the rating period concludes. Ensure employees with unacceptable performance are provided a reasonable opportunity to improve performance through counseling, training, closer supervision, and other appropriate measures during the reporting period. If this has been provided and the employee receives an "Unacceptable" rating then the employee's evaluation is forwarded to the

Reviewing Official or Review Board for final determination and personnel action.

(4) Encourage supervisors, managers, team leaders to nominate employees for awards who have shown an excellent standard of work performance, in accordance with reference(c), as soon as possible at the conclusion of the work performed. Awards are indicators used in the promotion of employees and for hiring purposes and should be awarded to employees as close to the work performed as practical.

(5) Train those employees who have supervisory or managerial responsibilities on the new performance management requirements.

    c. Supervisors, managers or team leaders will:

(1) Develop together as appropriate a written performance plan with each employee based on work assignments and responsibilities and provide the employee with a plan within 30 days of the beginning of the appraisal period. Each plan must include all critical elements and related performance standards. Each plan must have at least two critical elements addressing individual performance and each element must be rated as "Acceptable" or "Unacceptable". An "Unacceptable" in any one critical element will result in a summary rating of "Unacceptable". (See enclosure (3) for additional performance requirements).

(2) Provide one critical element for employees that are assigned to teams for individual performance on the team but not a team critical element.

(3) Provide employees that have supervisory or managerial duties with one critical element for each responsibility.

(4) Encourage employee participation and ensure each employee is involved in the development of their performance plan. Final responsibility for ensuring establishment of performance plans rests with the supervisor.

(5) Discuss training opportunities or rotational assignments for on-the-job training at the time the performance plan is written and include it in the plan so the employee will know what is expected of them to receive an "Acceptable" rating.

(6) Supervisors will discuss with those employees that normally meet or exceed the "Acceptable" level of performance, the many training opportunities available for developing as a

leader. For GS-7 through GS-15 and Wage Grade equivalent, supervisors will discuss the mentor program available in Civilian Leadership Development (CLD) at reference (e) and document the discussion on the supervisor's comment section of the appraisal form. An Individual Leadership Development Plan (ILDP) may be established if desired. The employee's mentor will be instrumental in the development of the ILDP. The supervisor or manager may be included in the development of the ILDP if the employee desires.

(7) Supervisors will conduct one or more documented progress reviews during the appraisal period. Progress reviews should be informative and developmental in nature and include discussions between the supervisor and team leader where applicable. Corrective actions should be discussed with the employee who does not meet "Acceptable" performance standards and a written plan of improvement shall be established with the employee.

(8) Supervisors will solicit input for the progress review and final summary rating from team leaders and other personnel both civilian and military that have contact with the employee regularly. The supervisor will have final responsibility for preparing the rating of record for each element and the assignment of a summary level. Discussions with team leaders on individual employee performance is highly recommended. A team rating is not to be given, only an individual performance rating for work performed as a team member. Both individual and team awards per references (c) and (d) should be considered for highly effective performance.

(9) Provide a copy of the approved rating of record to each employee as soon as practical.

(10) Provide assistance to employees in improving their performance at any time during the appraisal period if the performance is determined to be "Unacceptable" in one or more critical elements. The supervisor will counsel the employee on improving performance and set a written plan of action for improvement. The manager will ensure opportunities are provided by the supervisor for the employee to improve performance.

(11) Supervisors, team leaders, and managers should recommend incentive awards for employees whose performance surpasses the normal standards of "Acceptable", at any time during the reporting period and not just at the conclusion of the reporting period. References (c) and (d) should be used along with other personnel actions to reward excellent or superior performance. This is the most preferred method of distinguishing

the contributions of civilian employees as leaders in support of the Marine Corps mission, goals and objectives.

d. Covered employees will:

(1) Participate in the development of their performance plan and relevant individual training plans.

(2) Participate in a progress review(s) and cooperate with the supervisor or team leader to establish an individual plan for correction of performance deficiency. It is the responsibility of the individual employee to meet performance standards for each critical element established on the PARS.

(3) Provide input on their performance accomplishments at the end of the appraisal period and participate in the final appraisal discussion with the supervisor.

(4) Develop on a voluntary basis as part of Civilian Leadership Development an Individual Leadership Development Plan in accordance with reference (e). The mentor, supervisor or manager may assist the employee with the ILDP if the employee desires to participate in CLD.

e. Civilian Human Resource Offices (CHRO) currently served by an operational or regional Human Resource Service Center (HRSC) shall:

(1) Advise managers, supervisors, team leaders, and covered employees on program requirements and related performance management issues.

(2) Forward final close-out ratings and ratings of record to the HRSC for data input to the Defense Civilian Personnel Data System (DCPDS).

f. Additionally, HROs not currently served by an operational HRSC shall:

(1) Provide employee performance rating data to the DCPDS.

(2) Maintain performance records and forms and make them available for pay, awards, reduction-in-force, and other performance actions.

(3) Process awards and QSIs accurately and in a timely manner.

8. <u>Definitions</u>

a. <u>Acceptable Performance</u>. Performance of an employee which meets the established performance requirement(s) or standards, at a level above "Unacceptable," in all critical element(s) of an employee's position.

b. <u>Activity</u>. A field installation, headquarters command, or office.

c. <u>Additional Elements</u>. A dimension or aspect of individual, team, or organizational performance that is not a critical or non-critical element. Such elements are not used in assigning a summary level but, like critical and non-critical elements, are useful for purposes such as communicating performance expectations and serving as the basis for granting awards. Such elements include, but are not limited to, objectives, goals, program plans, individual work plans and other means of expressing performance.

d. <u>Appraisal</u>. The process under which performance is reviewed and evaluated against the described performance standards.

e. <u>Appraisal Period</u>. The established period of time for which performance will be reviewed and a rating of record prepared.

f. <u>Appraisal Program</u>. The specific procedures and requirements established within the policies and parameters of the DoD Performance Appraisal System.

g. <u>Appraisal System</u>. A framework of policies and procedures established by an agency for the administration of performance appraisal programs.

h. <u>Awards</u>. Recognition for individual or team achievement that contributes to meeting organizational goals or improving the efficiency, effectiveness, and economy of the Government or which is otherwise in the public interest.

i. <u>Close-out Rating</u>. An appraisal conducted when an employee or supervisor leaves a position after the employee has been under established performance standards for 90 days or more but before the end of the appraisal cycle. Close-out ratings will be documented and used in deriving the rating of record and in some cases, may become the rating of record.

j. <u>Critical Element</u>. A work assignment or responsibility of such importance that unacceptable performance on the element would result in a determination that an employee's overall performance is unacceptable.

k. <u>Interim Appraisal.</u> Any progress review or training appraisal conducted throughout the annual performance appraisal period.

l. <u>Non-critical Element</u>. Non-critical elements are not used in DON. Other Departments or Agencies do. Reference (a) applies.

m. v. Accomplishment of work assignments or responsibilities.

n. <u>Performance Plan</u>. All of the elements that describe the expected performance of an individual employee. A plan must include critical elements and their related performance standards.

o. <u>Performance Rating</u>. The results of a comparison between actual performance standards for each critical element on which there has been an opportunity to perform for the minimum period. A performance rating will include the assignment of a summary rating.

p. <u>Performance Standard.</u> The management-approved expression of the performance threshold(s), requirement(s), or expectation(s) that must be met to be appraised at a particular level of performance. A performance standard may include, but not limited to, quality, quantity, timeliness, and manner of performance.

q. <u>Progress Review</u>. Communicating with the employee about performance compared to the performance standards of critical elements.

r. <u>Rating of Record.</u> The performance rating prepared at the end of an appraisal period for performance over the entire period including the assignment of a summary level. The rating of record is the official rating for pay, performance award, and retention purposes.

s. <u>Summary Rating</u>. The final result of the performance evaluation process. The summary rating is used to provide consistency in describing ratings of record. The two summary rating levels are: "Acceptable" and "Unacceptable".

t. <u>Training Appraisal.</u> An appraisal conducted as part of a formal training program, lasting more than 90 days, and conducted under Civilian Personnel Instruction (CPI) 410. Training appraisals are interim appraisals and are not used as the annual rating of record.

u. <u>Unacceptable Performance</u>. Performance of an employee which fails to meet established performance standards in one or more critical elements.

9. <u>Performance Appraisal Requirements</u>

a. <u>General Requirements</u>

(1) No employee may be concurrently covered by more than one performance appraisal program.

(2) An annual appraisal period is required for rating of record purposes on each employee. The reporting period is established by the activity head or commander where applicable.

b. <u>Performance Plans</u>

(1) Individual performance plans are required for each employee. Plans will be written and based on work assignments and responsibilities. The plan will cover the official appraisal period.

(2) Individual performance plans will be provided to employees within 30 days after the beginning of each appraisal period, permanent assignment to a new position, and of each detail or temporary promotion expected to last a 120 days or longer. Performance plans include all critical elements and related performance standards.

(3) Each performance plan must have at least two critical elements which address individual performance. Examples are provided at enclosure (1). In addition, the performance plans are to include the critical elements required for specific types of positions, such as safety, security, and those found in enclosure (3).

(4) One of two summary rating levels must be used for the final performance rating, either "Acceptable " or "Unacceptable".

(5) When performance standards are set, supervisors and employees must certify that this has been done on the appraisal form. Supervisors must also certify the employees position description is accurate at the time standards are set. If the

position description is not accurate the supervisor must take action to rewrite it within 60 days.

    c. <u>Monitoring Performance</u>

       (1) <u>Progress Reviews</u>. A review of an employee's performance is expected at least once midway through the appraisal period. At a minimum, a comparison will be made with the performance elements and standards established. To the maximum extent possible, progress reviews will be informative and developmental in nature and will focus on future performance. Progress reviews do not require the assignment of a summary level, however, the supervisor and employee must sign and date the performance appraisal to indicate the review was conducted.

       (2) <u>Interim Appraisals.</u> These should be conducted throughout the annual performance appraisal period. Interim appraisals are considered in determining the annual rating of record.

       (3) <u>Training Appraisals</u>. These are conducted under CPI 410 covering periods of at least 90 days. Training appraisals should be considered in the annual performance rating process. These ratings are not considered close-out ratings of record.

       (4) <u>Close-out Ratings</u>. These must be conducted when:

          (a) An employee completes a detail or temporary promotion of 120 days or longer under established performance standards. This requirement also applies to employees on loan from another activity/agency for 120 days or longer.

          (b) An employee changes positions, is promoted, or moves to a new agency/activity, after being under established performance standards a minimum of 90 days.

          (c) The supervisor leaves the position after the employee is under established performance standards for a minimum of 90 days. In this situation, the employee may continue under the same performance plan unless changed by the new supervisor.

          (d) Close-out ratings may become the rating of record if the following criteria are met:

             <u>1</u> There is insufficient time (90 days) to establish a new performance plan and rate the covered employee in their assigned position before the end of the appraisal period.

             <u>2</u> The supervisor takes into consideration any other close-out ratings conducted during the appraisal period.

(5) <u>Rating of Record</u>

(a) Normally within 30 days after the end of the appraisal period, a written rating of record will be given to each employee, unless the employee has not completed the 90 day minimum period of performance.

(b) When a rating of record cannot be prepared at the time specified, the appraisal period will be extended to insure the minimum 90 day period. A rating of record should be prepared as soon as practicable once the necessary conditions have been met.

(c) The rating of record or performance rating for a disabled veteran will not be lowered because the veteran has been absent from work to seek medical treatment.

(6) <u>Summary Level Rating</u>. A summary level rating must be assigned when a performance rating is prepared as part of a rating of record.

(a) Ratings are based on a comparison of performance against written standards. Each critical element is rated at the "Acceptable" or "Unacceptable" level.

(b) An "Unacceptable summary rating level is assigned if, and only if, performance on one or more critical elements is appraised as "Unacceptable."

(7) <u>Recording the Results</u>

(a) The performance rating shall be signed and dated by the employee and immediate supervisor. The employee's signature does not constitute agreement with the rating; it merely signifies that the employee has received it.

(b) Employees should be provided a copy of their rating of record within 60 days of the end of the annual appraisal period. Timeliness is important in order for supervisors to establish new individual performance plans, for employee promotions and applying for new positions.

10. <u>"Unacceptable" Performance</u>

a. At any time during the appraisal period that performance is determined to be "Unacceptable" in one or more critical elements, <u>employees are to be formally notified in writing</u>. The notice of unacceptable performance must include:

(1) The critical element(s) determined to be unacceptable;

(2) The performance requirement(s) and acceptable standard that must be attained to demonstrate acceptable performance;

(3) A reasonable opportunity to demonstrate acceptable performance;

(4) Assistance in improving performance which may include, but is not limited to, formal training, on-the-job training, counseling, close supervision or other appropriate measures; and

(5) Notice to the employee that unless performance in the critical element(s) improves and is sustained at the acceptable level, the employee will be reassigned, reduced in grade or removed.

b. A rating of record of "Unacceptable" may not be assigned until the above requirements have been met. If, at the conclusion of the opportunity period, the employee's performance continues to be "Unacceptable," the activity must initiate reassignment, reduction in grade, or removal action.

c. A rating of record of "Unacceptable" shall be reviewed and approved by a Reviewing Official or Review Board.

11. <u>Grievances and Appeals</u>. Covered employees may raise issues relating to the performance appraisal process through either the administrative grievance procedure or, where applicable, a negotiated grievance procedure. Appealable issues may be submitted to the Merit Systems Protection Board (MSPB). Guidance on grievable/appealable matters is as follows:

a. Contents of the individual performance plan are neither grievable nor appealable.

b. Failure to inform employees of critical elements and standards within the required time frame is grievable.

c. Ratings on individual elements and summary level ratings are grievable.

d. Performance based demotions and removals may be grieved through the appropriate negotiated grievance procedure or appealed to the MSPB, but not both.

e.   Awards are not grievable under administrative grievance procedures.

12.   <u>Performance Recognition</u>

a.   <u>Awards</u>.   Awards may be used as tools to acknowledge and motivate employees by recognizing and rewarding significant individual, team, organizational achievements or contributions.   Examples of awards include, but not limited to, special act awards, time-off, honorary and informal recognition awards.   References (c) and (d) apply.

b.   <u>Quality Step Increase</u>.   The purpose of the QSI is to provide appropriate incentives and recognition for excellence in performance by granting faster than normal step increases; therefore, careful consideration should be given before granting a QSI.   An employee is eligible for only one QSI within any 52 week period.   To be eligible for a QSI, General Schedule employees must meet the following criteria:

(1) Receive a rating of record of "Acceptable."

(2) Employee demonstrates a sustained performance of high quality significantly above that expected at the "Acceptable" level, depicting unusually good, excellent quality or higher quantity of work provided ahead of schedule and with less than normal supervision.

(3) Employee makes a significant contribution to the organization's mission.

(4) There must be an expectation that the high quality performance will continue in the future.

13.   <u>Relationship to Other Personnel Actions</u>

a.   <u>Within-Grade Increases</u>

(1) <u>Federal Wage System (FWS)</u>.   Employees receive within-grade increases, when eligible by time, if their performance is satisfactory. Satisfactory performance equates to an "Acceptable" rating of record.

(2) <u>General Schedule (GS)</u>.   Covered employees receive within-grade increases, when eligible by time, if their performance is at an acceptable level of competence.   Acceptable level of competence equates to an "Acceptable" rating of record.

(3) <u>FWS and GS</u>.   When a within-grade increase decision is not consistent with the employee's most recent rating of

record, a new rating of record must be prepared. The rating of record used as the basis for an acceptable level of competence determination for a within-grade increase must have been assigned no earlier than the most recently completed appraisal period. The notice of negative within-grade increase determination must state the "Acceptable" standard for any element evaluated at the "Unacceptable" level.

    b. <u>Promotions</u>

        (1) <u>Career-Ladder Promotions.</u> Performance appraisals are used as a basis for determining eligibility for career-ladder promotions. To be promoted, an employee is expected to be performing at the Acceptable" level on all critical elements. However, an "Acceptable" rating does not mean an automatic promotion.

        (2) <u>Merit Promotions</u>. The rating of record should be used in merit promotion evaluations and by selecting officials to the extent it is relevant to the position to be filled.

    c. <u>Probationary Period</u>

        (1) <u>Initial Probationary Period</u>. Evaluation of the employee's performance, as well as other considerations, should serve as a basis for the decision to retain or remove the employee from Federal service during the probationary period.

        (2) <u>Supervisory and Managerial Probation.</u> Evaluation of the employee's performance of supervisory or managerial elements of the position serves as a basis for the decision to retain or remove the employee from the supervisory or managerial position.

    d. <u>Removal, Demotion, and Reassignment</u>

        (1) An employee whose performance is "Unacceptable" must be removed, reassigned, or reduced in grade, but only after the employee has had an opportunity to demonstrate acceptable performance.

        (2) If, at the conclusion of the opportunity period, the employee's performance continues to be "Unacceptable" the activity must initiate reassignment, reduction in grade, or removal.

    e. <u>Reduction-in-Force</u>

        (1) The rating of record for RIF purposes is the annual rating conducted at the time specified by the activity and special ratings conducted to support within-grade increase

determinations. No rating may be assigned for the purpose of affecting an employee's RIF retention standing.

        (2) The three most recent ratings of record received in the last four years are factors in determining retention standing for RIF purposes. An employee receives an additional 20 years of service for each "Acceptable" or satisfactory rating from other rating systems.

        (3) For the purpose of determining the Service Computation Date for reduction-in-force (RIF), an employee with an "Acceptable" rating will receive 20 years of credit when a "mixed system" exists. A "mixed system" is one in which an employee has ratings of record for the last three years from a performance management system using 3, 4, or 5 levels along with a rating of record from a two level system. For example: A RIF is planned in the G-1 organization. One employee in the G-1 organization, came from Agency X where a three level system was used. This employee has one "Acceptable" rating of record under the Marine Corps two level system and two ratings of "Out- standing" under a three level system. In this case we have a "mixed system" situation. In a "mixed system" three level situation, all ratings above the satisfactory level will receive 20 years of credit. Thus in the example cited above, the employee from Agency X would receive 20 years of credit for each rating of "Outstanding" and 20 years of credit from the Marine Corps' "Acceptable" rating. See the element rating conversion chart at enclosure (4) to convert elements to summary rating.

        (4) When only a two level system is used for calculations for RIF, 20 years is credited for "Acceptable" for Service Computation Date.

        (5) In a three level system, 20 years of credit is given for satisfactory or above for Service Computation Date.

        (6) In a four level system, 20 years of credit is given only for the top two levels, satisfactory or above, for the Service Computation Date.

        (7) No credit is given for Minimally Successful or below in a five level system. Only the top three levels, Fully Successful (12 years of credit), Exceeds Fully Successful (16 years credit) and Outstanding (20 years credit), will be calculated for Service Computation Date.

    f. Training and Development

        (1) Identification of training requirements to improve performance is a significant element in the appraisal process.

The performance appraisal process should clearly identify areas where training and development may be appropriate. Whenever it is determined an employee's performance is "Unacceptable" the supervisor is responsible for assisting the employee in bringing his or her performance to the "Acceptable" level. (See paragraph 10a(4) of this Order.)

(2) Performance plans related to training may include achievement of specific training objectives that may be determined to be critical or additional. Performance appraisals conducted as part of the employee's individual training plan or their specialized training plan should be considered in the annual performance rating process. Such appraisals are interim appraisals and do not serve as the rating of record.

14. <u>Transfer of Rating.</u> When an employee's Official Personnel Folder (OPF) is sent to another servicing office in the employing agency, another agency, or the National Personnel Records Center, all ratings of record completed in the previous four year period, as well as the performance plan on which the most recent rating was based, are to be included in the OPF. Activities should take into consideration transferred ratings covering an employee's performance within their current appraisal period when deriving the next rating of record.

J. W. KLIMP
Deputy Chief of Staff for
Manpower and Reserve Affairs

Distribution: PCN 10212055100

   Copy to: 7000110 (50)
             7000111 (20)
             7000027 (20)

17

UNITED STATES MARINE CORPS
PERFORMANCE APPRAISAL REVIEW SYSTEM

PART 1

NAME OF EMPLOYEE	SOCIAL SECURITY NUMBER
POSITION TITLE	SERIES AND GRADE
LOCATION OF EMPLOYEE (DIVISION/SECTION)	RATING PERIOD

RECORD OF REVIEWS AND FINAL APPRAISAL

	STANDARDS DATE	PROGRESS REVIEW DATE	FINAL RATING DATE
SUPERVISOR			
EMPLOYEE			
REVIEWING OFFICIAL (UNACCEPTABLE ONLY)			

☐ RATING OF RECORD   ☐ INTERIM APPRAISAL

☐ ACCEPTABLE   ☐ UNACCEPTABLE

EMPLOYEE'S POSITION DESCRIPTION IS CURRENT AND ACCURATE?

☐ YES   ☐ NO

If NO, then the supervisor will rewrite Position Description within 60 days.

CRITICAL ELEMENTS

ELEMENTS	RATING	A	U

MCO 12430.2
29 DEC 1998

ELEMENTS	CRITICAL ELEMENTS		
	RATING	A	U

NAVMC 11408 (9-98) (EF)
SN: 0109-LF-070-1500

Designed Using FormFlow 2.15, HQMC/ARAE Sep 98

COMMENTS OF SUPERVISOR

	YES	NO	NOT APPLICABLE
The opportunities in Civilian Leadership Development (CLD) have been discussed with the employee.	☐	☐	☐
An Individual Leadership Development Plan (ILDP) has been initiated by the employee and their mentor.	☐	☐	☐

3   ENCLOSURE (1)

NAVMC 11408 (9-98) (EF)
SN: 0109-LF-070-1500

Designed Using FormFlow 2.15, HQMC/ARAE Sep 98

EXAMPLES OF CRITICAL ELEMENTS

1. Element #1 - Execution of Duties

Completes work assignments in a timely manner, assuring a quality of work that meets the needs of the unit goals and objectives or Division mission. Develops solutions to problems which demonstrate improvement in work methods. Supports and conforms to policy, procedures and regulations.

2. ELEMENT #2 - Team Activities

Takes positive action to promote teamwork and takes responsibility either in a leadership or support role. Productively works on goals and objectives.

3. ELEMENT #3 - Communications

Presents written and oral communications in a clear, correct, timely and understandable manner; keeps supervisor and/or coworkers informed of issues and problems; provides information and guidance that is correct and according to regulations.

4. ELEMENT #4 - Research and Analysis

Thoroughly and accurately researches issues in a timely manner, using appropriate reference sources. Makes reasonable recommendations or decisions based on available guidance.

5. ELEMENT #5 - Organizational Support

Provides recommendations that are timely, responsive and accurate. Maintains rapport with internal and external divisions, agencies or organizations. Develops and establishes work relationships with external organizations, as required. Keeps supervisor and/or team leader informed of difficult and/or controversial issues and unique problems. Takes action to effectively solve problems before they have an adverse impact on the organization or other employees.

6. ELEMENT #6 - Skills Maintenance

Maintains an adequate level of skill to perform duties and seeks training or on the job training to increase level of competency as necessary for performance of assigned tasks.

7. ELEMENT #7 - Personal Contacts

Demonstrates courteous and tactful behavior towards internal and external organizations, coworkers, supervisors, team members

1

and subordinates. Projects a positive and professional image of the Marine Corps at all times.

8. ELEMENT #8 - Resource Management (use for managers)

Monitors allocated funds and maintains complete and accurate records of expenditures. Utilizes resources in an efficient and effective manner. Ensures that funds, property, and other resources are guarded against fraud, waste, loss, unauthorized use and misappropriation.

9. ELEMENT #9 - Equal Employment Opportunity (use for managers, supervisors, or team leaders)

Applies principles of equal opportunity. Selects individuals for team activities, for recruitment, promotion, and training without regard to non-merit factors. Assigns work in an equitable manner, without regard to sex, race, national origin, religion, personal favoritism, age, marital status, political affiliation. Promptly investigates allegations of discrimination and takes appropriate corrective action if allegations are founded.

10. ELEMENT #10 - Supervision (use for supervisors or managers)

Assigns work fairly and in a manner productive for the organization. Provides policy guidance including goals and objectives to staff. Gives timely technical guidance to subordinate staff to support accomplishment of tasks or objectives. Supports and implements management decisions. Corrects performance and conduct problems promptly and fairly. Ensures staff is properly trained and complies with occupational safety and health regulations.

11. ELEMENT #11 - Program/Project Management (use for managers or team leaders)

Manages program/project resolving issues and problems that arise in the administration of such. Monitors all aspects of program/project quality, efficiency and consistency. Establishes program/project plans and guidance in response to objectives, requirements, specifications and regulations. Ensures policy instructions to staff/team are accurate and clearly understood. Completes work within time constraints or on schedule. Evaluates effectiveness of work performed and adjusts plans accordingly. Reports progress of work accomplished to director or head of organization as required.

ENCLOSURE (2)

12.   ELEMENT #12 - Special Projects (use for team members or team leader)

    Special projects are supported with research and active participation in work assignments. Integrates special projects into workload and completes work on time without causing team/work delay or disruption. Team leader provides clear instructions, monitors team members progress on objectives and provides reports as required. Special assignments are completed independently or in collaboration with others to ensure quality. Team Leader ensures that project complies with regulations and procedures.

ADDITIONAL PERFORMANCE REQUIREMENTS

1. Purpose. Specific provisions of law, regulation, and DoD policy require certain matters to be considered in the performance evaluations of some employees. Except as provided below, this does not require the establishment of specific performance elements and standards addressing the individual's performance. Rating officials may just consider these requirements in the performance rating or provide narrative evaluations of progress in meeting these requirements.

2. DoD Performance Evaluation Requirements

   a. Audit Follow-up. Performance evaluations of appropriate managers must reflect the degree of effectiveness in addressing audit findings, recommendations, and implementing agreed-upon corrective actions as required by Office of Management and Budget (OMB) Circular A-50, "Audit Follow-up", September 29, 1982. This requirement applies to audits conducted by the General Accounting Office (GAO) and the DoD Inspector General. This requirement is established in paragraph E3g of DoD Directive 7650.3, "Follow-up on General Accounting Office, DoD Inspector General Internal Audit, and Internal Review Reports", September 5, 1989.

   b. Protecting Classified Information. Performance evaluations of all employees whose duties involve access to classified information must include a comment by rating officials pertaining to an employee's discharge of security responsibilities. This requirement is established in paragraph 9-102(d) of DoD 5200.2-R, "Personnel Security Program", January 1987.

   c. Internal Management Control. Performance evaluations of managers who have significant Internal Management Control (IMC) responsibilities must reflect the accountability for the success or failure of IMC practices. This requirement is established in paragraph E3d of DoD Directive 5101.39, "Internal management Control Program", April 14, 1987.

   d. Equal Employment Opportunity (EEO). Performance evaluations of supervisors, managers, and other personnel with EEO responsibilities must have a critical element on EEO. This requirement is established in paragraph E2f of DoD Directive 1440.1, "The DoD Equal employment Opportunity (EEO) Program", May 21, 1987.

   e. Inventory Management. Performance evaluations of individuals employed at Inventory Control Points must give appropriate consideration to efforts made by these individuals to

1

eliminate wasteful practices and achieve cost savings in the acquisition and management of inventory items. This requirement is established in section 2458 of Title 10, United States Code.

f. Acquisitions. Persons serving in acquisition positions in the same acquisition career field must be provided an opportunity for review and inclusion of any comments on any appraisal of the performance of a person serving in an acquisition position. This requirement is established in paragraph D19 of DoD Directive 5000.52, "Defense Acquisition Education, Training, and Career Development Program", October 25, 1991.

g. Regulatory Reinvention. Performance measurements of persons who are front line regulators, (i.e., those who have authority to order a corrective action or levy a fine on a business or other government entity), must focus on results, not based on process and punishment. Therefore, such measures should not be based on process (e.g., number of visits to a business or government entity) or punishment (e.g., number of violations found, number of fines levied on a business or government entity). This requirement is established by a Presidential Memorandum for heads of Federal departments and agencies, "Classified National Security Information", March 4, 1995.

h. Classified Information Management. The performance ratings of civilian employees who are original classification authorities, security managers or security specialists, or significantly involved in the creation or handling of classified information must include the management of classified information as a critical element or item to be evaluated. This requirement is established in section 56(c)(7) of Executive Order 12958, "Classified National Security Information," April 17, 1995.

i. Safety. Responsible DoD officials at each management level, including first level supervisors, must to the extent of their authority, comply with the DoD Occupational Safety and Health Program guidance and regulations. Performance evaluations of those employees must reflect personal accountability in this respect, consistent with the duties of the position, with appropriate recognition of superior performance, and conversely, with corrective administrative action, as appropriate, for deficient performance. This requirement is established in enclosure (2) to DoD Instruction 6055.1, "DoD Occupational Safety and Health Program," October 26, 1984.

ENCLOSURE (3)

j. <u>Increased Competition and Cost Savings in Contracts</u>.
Performance evaluations of officials involved in contracting and

acquisition must give appropriate recognition to efforts to increase
competition and achieve cost savings. This requirement is established
in section 2317 of Title 10, United States Code.

ELEMENTS RATING CONVERSION CHART
EXAMPLES

The following examples translate element ratings into summary ratings using 2, 3, 4, 5, levels. Element ratings can have multi-levels but must translate into a summary rating of "Acceptable" or "Unacceptable".

ELEMENT RATING	SUMMARY RATING
Outstanding Exceeds Fully Successful Fully Successful	Acceptable
Minimally Successful Unacceptable	Unacceptable
Above Fully Successful Fully Successful	Acceptable
Below Fully Successful	Unacceptable
Pass	Acceptable
Fail	Unacceptable

1

ENCLOSURE (4)

www.ingramcontent.com/pod-product-compliance
Lightning Source LLC
Chambersburg PA
CBHW080747290526
45790CB00008B/3352